PARTS

Subpersonalities, Conflicting Desires, & Christian Thought

Erik Douglas Johnson

Parts
Subpersonalities, Conflicting Desires, & Christian Thought

1st edition, June 2009
2nd edition, April, 2018

St. Whimsy Publications
Erik Johnson
1780 Harksell Road
Ferndale, WA 98248

ISBN-13: 978-1986745345
ISBN-10: 1986745341

www.ErikDouglasJohnson.com

Dedicated to Dr. Mitch Whitman
Scholar, therapist, mentor, friend, brother

*"Bei denen aber wird Freude sein,
die zum Frieden raten."*
Sprüche 12,20

*"Der, der mit den Weisen
umgeht, wird weise."*
Sprüche 13,20

Contents

Introduction

Many who come into our counseling office have one thing in common, a desire for greater self-control. With greater self-control these teenagers, men and women would:

- Criticize, nag, and provoke their family less
- Rage at, badger, and harangue their friends less
- Stay calm when rejected by family and friends
- Be patient with noisy, messy, and defiant children
- Endure irritating coworkers with grace
- Quit the gambling, drinking, porn, or drug habit
- Quit procrastinating and make tough decisions
- Lose weight, gain weight, accept their weight
- Quit collecting injustices, quit keeping score
- Be less competitive, less aggressive, less driven
- Stop trying to control people and circumstances
- Overcome envy, judging, and gossip
- Overcome anger, self sabotaging behaviors
- Overcome prejudice, suspicion, and pride
- Be bold, courageous, and more assertive
- Control temper in traffic, meetings, or at home
- Take the school classes they've been avoiding
- Hunker down, study, and earn better grades

"I am determined to break my bad habits!!"

Erik Douglas Johnson

- Improve job skills
- Start that novel, children's book, or memoir
- Stop pining for ex-lovers
- Overcome shyness
- Overcome anxiety
- Overcome depression
- Stop writing bad checks
- Kick the gambling habit
- Live within a budget
- Stop hating offenders from the past
- Write a new resume
- Disengage from toxic friends
- React less when things go wrong
- Declutter the house
- Watch less TV
- Set boundaries with difficult people
- Change negative thinking patterns
- Quit visiting certain web sites
- Quit hurting themselves
- Conquer obsessive thoughts, fears, and worries
- Quit being a perfectionist
- Manage hard-to-control moods
- Overcome defensiveness and dereliction of duty
- Avoid conflict escalation patterns
- Apply conflict reduction skills
- And more.

Imagine what we could do if we all had greater self control. The benefits are endless! So why don't we have greater self control? Why is it so hard to get our will to cooperate with our hopes and dreams for a different future?

Because we misunderstand of the parts of our heart. Our hearts have subconscious urges and desires that overpower us. These parts hi-jack our brain and drive us off a cliff. We have addictions and cravings that are hard to control. We have obsessive thoughts and compulsive behaviors. We are lead by knee-jerk feelings and tormented by purposes in our heart we neither recognize or understand. No matter what we say or do we seem to make matters worse and we can't stop ourselves.

> *"The mind…is a quite complicated aspect of the person, with numerous subdivisions built into both thought and feeling."*
>
> Dallas Willard, **Renovation of the Heart**, page 33.

Our minds conjure images that entice, and fears that paralyze. When we stop to think about it, the things that go on inside our hearts are very puzzling!

It's been my privilege as a counselor for the last twenty years to help people understand the parts of their heart, explain what each part does, how those parts relate to each other, and how to tame and coordinate them all.

My ambition in this book is to coach readers by speaking in plain English, simplifying complex ideas, and making the steps to self control as accessible as possible. When I do my work well, clients (and now readers) work hard, the results are astonishing.

In the chapters to come you'll read stories of men, women, children, and teenagers who learned about the different parts of their heart and then applied the steps to coordinate them. Many achieved a level of self control they didn't know was possible.

Now, I don't want to oversell these ideas, so in the spirit of full disclosure here's my truth in advertising blurb. Understanding the parts of our heart is not a miracle cure for instant self control. Some clients did not benefit from these notions. Either the temptations were too strong, or the client's core self wasn't strong enough yet, or my coaching was too weak.

I would love to create a silver bullet therapy that heals all emotional pain, untangles all those stuck on the horns of a dilemma, cures all thorny relational conflicts, and breaks my bad habit of mixing metaphors.

*"Here's another Instant Self Control
book you can filed under fiction!"*

I'd love to write a book entitled **Complete Self Control Made Really Easy**. But I can't.

The results of self control coaching are so unpredictable that I first thought to call this book, **Partial Self Control Made Only Sort Of Easy**.

Applying these ideas is not super-duper easy (although I'll describe how as clearly as possible). Those who invest the effort will gain some but not complete self control. So if, Mr. and Ms. Reader, you're looking for a surefire cure for all the mental confusion occurring in your fertile cerebrum, if you want something with guaranteed results over addiction and obsessions on the order of chemical or mathematical precision, and if you picked up this book for maximum outcome with minimal effort, I can't help you. Sorry.

On the other hand, the breakthroughs that many clients have enjoyed compel me to make these ideas available to everyone. Despite its lack of 100% effectiveness, I still feel delight when clients with troubled minds and stubborn habits enjoy positive outcomes.

• A man with a thirty year lust problem said after one session, *"I've had more freedom this past week than I have in years."*

• A woman in her 50s with chronic self-criticism said, *"I can't believe it. For the first time ever I've talked back to my critical part and weakened its grip."*

• A 12 year old boy reports, *"I named my fear part 'Aaa!' and whenever I'm afraid, I tell Aaa, 'You're not the boss of me!' and Aaa backs down."* His parents validate the positive changes this formerly fear-driven boy now enjoys.

Behind these stories and many more is this idea: even though we've got one body and inside it one heart (or said another way, we've got one head and one brain) the heart comes with many parts. Those parts are not the real us, not our core self, not the inner spirit where the real you dwells. Those parts are in our soul, some so strong they have a mind of their own. They are often hard to manage, defiant and unwilling to yield their power without a fight.

Parts: Subpersonalities Conflicting Desires & Christian Thought means that with hard work we can have victory over many of those bossy, hard to manage parts. In the pages that follow we'll show you how.

PART I

What's New In The Parts Department?

One

We've All Got Parts

A client who loved to work on cars enjoyed my opening question each week, *"What's new in the parts department?"* He had learned about his self-destructive parts and knew we were going to evaluate his progress at managing them.

This is what I want for readers of this book.

Everything is made up of parts. A team has many players, an engine has many components, and even a single cell amoeba has many biochemical properties.

Our nation's motto, *"E Pluribus Unum"* means "out of the one, many."

One human body has many parts—eyes, mouth, hands, feet, etc..

What's true for teams, engines, amoebas, nations, and even our bodies is true of our heart as well.

But because this idea is not entirely self evident some people require extra convincing. There are good reasons why people find this idea challenging.

The parts of our heart are so intricately woven together it feels like we are a unitary, solitary, simple being. Not so. Having many parts in our hearts is counter intuitive.

Talking about multiple parts conjures fear of Multiple Personality Disorder or Dissociative Identity Disorder. The whole idea seems unfamiliar and even a little spooky.

There are so many invisible parts in the heart with so many complex and confusing definitions that it is easier to mush them all together into one amorphous blob and simply call it, *"Myself."*

Psychologists have come up with a theory of parts of our heart called subpersonalities. Many are wary of anything cooked up by psychologists. So, a preliminary step in learning about self control is believing that the heart really has parts. If you're already convinced of this you can jump to Part II and begin the work of managing your parts. But if you're like many, Part 1 **What's New in the Parts Department** is for those who need some convincing.

"It was the best of times and it was the worst of times." Charles Dickens in **A Tale of Two Cities** recognized one era could be two things at once. Like us!

When I first mention parts clients ask three questions.

1. *"Are you saying I've got subpersonalities, entities in my heart trying to take over? Yikes!"*
2. *"Are you saying I've got Multiple Personality Disorder?"*
3. *Do you trust science?*

My answer to is, *"Yes," "No,"* and *"Yes."*

Those are my short answers. The next couple of chapters will be my long answers to convince doubters that our hearts do indeed have many parts.

Seashells have parts

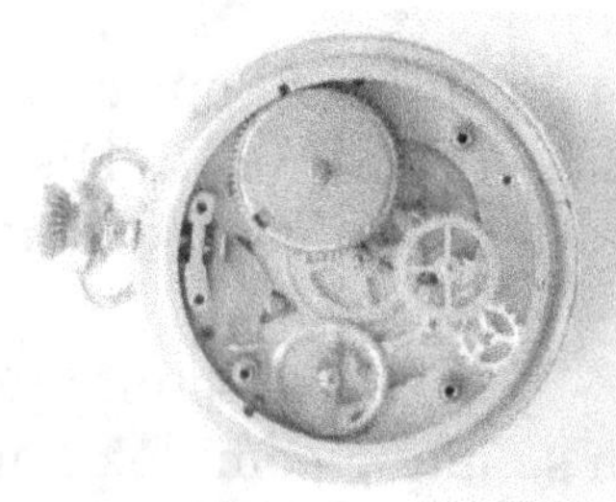

Watches have parts

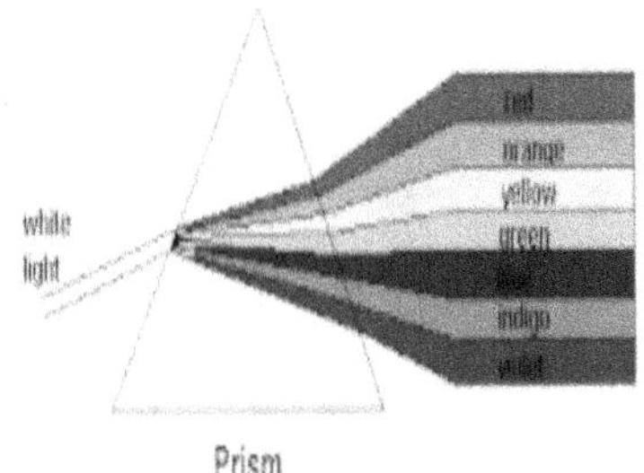

White light has parts

Cell phones
have parts

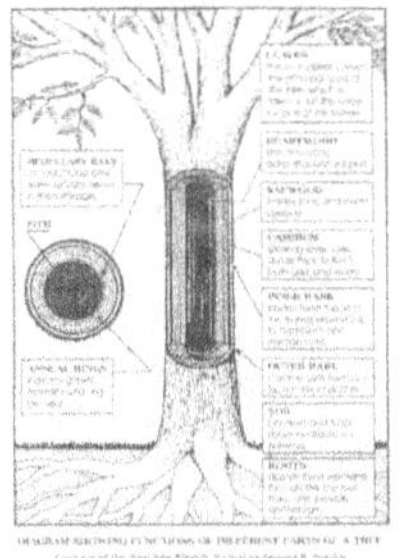

Trees have parts

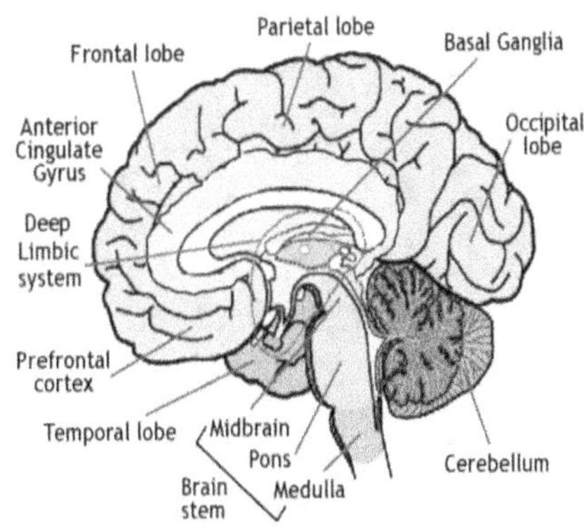

Brains have parts

Two
The Experience
Proof of Parts

*"Are you saying I've got subpersonalities,
entities in my heart trying to take over? Yikes?!"*

Yes. *"Subpersonalities"* is the name given by
psychologists to describe different parts of our thinking, different aspects of our personalities. I prefer the
term *"parts"* and use it with clients and will use it in
these pages.

The parts in our heart have unique patterns of
perceiving the world, unique ways of relating to and
thinking about life, have different purposes from other parts, and are different from our core self (also
known by some as the soul, spirit, inner being, or true
self).

Some parts, due to trauma, past disappoint-
ments, or emotional hurt, are wounded and hide in
the shadows never wanting to be hurt again. Their
goal: Avoid pain.

Some parts adopt the role of protector, doing all
they can to make sure the wounded part never gets
hurt again. When pain is threatened our protector

*"I'm a committee. Actually, I have a committee, but it
often acts as if it's in charge. If I could just get my
inner management committee into consensus—or
shut up—I'd probably never experience stress."*

David Allen, **Ready for Anything,** pages 103-104.

parts act out with perfectionism, control, people pleasing, wanting to be liked, care taking, conflict voidance, obsessive worry, and want to look good to others. Their goal? Prevent pain.

Still other parts act out when pain is triggered: they're the parts who prompt eating disorders, cutting, suicidal thoughts, numbing out with substance abuse. They say, *"I'll do anything as long as it stops the pain, and I don't care who gets hurt in the process."*

Unless parts are well-managed, they take control and negatively influence our thoughts and behaviors. Parts are not second persons living inside us, but are discreet (separate from each other) and unique (with their own idiosyncrasies).

Treat your parts as another living personality trait, with ideas of their own that are different from your core self.

The following experiences will illustrate how common this notion of parts is.

1. Buyer's remorse. We eagerly sign on the dotted line for a new car. The next day we bite our nails and wail, *"What have I done?!"* Part #1 loved buying the new car, Part #2 is worried, fearful, and full of regret.

2. Simultaneous contradictory feelings. Do these experiences sound familiar?
"I am excited about marriage; I'm afraid of marriage."
"I am happy to quit my job; I am sad to quit my job."
"I want to confront that person who hurt me; I am reluctant to do so."

"I am proud of my choices; I am ashamed of my choices."
"I am determined to quit this bad habit; I can't wait to do it again."
"I am excited about going to this party; I'd rather stay home and read."
"My spirit is willing; at the same time my flesh is weak."

"My brain tells me one thing; my heart tells me another."
"My brain has a mind of its own."
"I'm torn between two sides."
"No one can tell me what to do, even myself!"
"I'm betwixt and between!"

These are parts disagreeing with each other.

3. Flexible personalities. If you're like me, you act one way in your professional life and a different way at home. Come on now, be honest. I know we say we value transparency and consistency and that we don't care what others think. But how many of us dance around the office in our pajamas like we do at home, or treat our kids like employees like we do at work? When we hang out with our baseball lovin' friends we're all stats and scores. But at our kid's open house we talk to teachers with our academic hat on. Different roles bring out different parts.

4. Chorus of critical voices. How can a nice person like you have such negative thoughts about yourself? Okay, okay, I admit it. I don't know for sure that you have self-critical thoughts. But I do. My inner critic calls me names, makes me feel bad, empty, worthless.

And most of those in my office at times have parts that call them names like, *"Dummy," "Lame brain," "Idiot."* Where do those negative thoughts come from? Parts. Nasty ones. Some parts judge us continuously,

whatever we do or say. It's like having a nonstop internal critic in our head scolding us constantly.

5. Defending family. How is it we can criticize our kids or our partner but if someone else does it we come unglued? Because one part plays the role of family critic while another part plays the role of family protector. Two roles, two parts.

6. Indecision. When presented with two very good options it is not always clear which option is best. Why not? One part thinks option A is best and another part thinks option B is best. The two of them duke it out until one comes out the victor. Voila! Parts at work.

7. Talking to one's self. It seems so obvious now. As a lifelong talking-out-loud-to-myself kind of guy, I recognize that talking to myself is really just my parts discussing various topics. Thinking is merely our parts talking to each other. When I make a promise to myself, it is one part of me telling another part of me, *"Keep you word."* Note: one advantage of embracing multiple parts—we're never alone!

8. Pairs of human quips. Ever notice how certain sayings have opposites?
- He who hesitates is lost/Look before you leap.
- Beware of Greeks bearing gifts/Don't look a gift horse in the mouth.
- Look after pennies and the dollars will take care of

themselves/You can't take it with you.

- A stitch in time saves nine/Haste makes waste.

How can these opposite sayings all be true? Because different parts of our experience seem true in some contexts and not true in others. Parts at work!

9. Neurology. The left/right hemisphere model of brain science is incomplete. Turns out there aren't only two but many parts of our brain with exotic sounding names like left inferior prefrontal cortex, hippocampus, perietal lobes, and our old friend the amygdala. Each serves a different function—memory, decision making, processing and regulating emotions, calculating, and so forth. Each part is doing different work. Getting them coordinated is one definition of mental health. Incoherent parts leads to an incoherent life. When parts are fragmented we say, *"I'm falling apart!"*

10. Boredom. One of the more fascinating aspects of human motivation is boredom. How can we get enthusiastic about some project, hobby, movie, job, or interest and then lose interest so quickly? One part gets enthusiastic about something then another part says, *"This isn't as interesting as I thought."* Qohelet had this problem in Ecclesiastes. He got all ramped up doing different projects, convinced that they would satisfy him. They didn't. Qohelet's other part took over and said, *"This is vanity!"*

11. *"I'm just not myself."* Those with personality changes due to depression, guilt, shame, or fear know what I'm talking about. We were happy go lucky, now we're down in the dumps. We were resilient and upbeat. Now we're on edge. We sabotage relationships, blurt out things we regret, give up on dreams we've worked on for months, and oversleep when we need to get up. That is parts doing their often diabolical work!

"Though always the same woman, Cleopatra was alternatively lover, friend, cool, hot, temptress, enemy, submissive, and demanding. One person can be many."

Peter Bernstein
Against the Gods, page 157

12. Social groups. A teacher says, *"Your child is such a delight to have in class,"* and we think, *"Are we talking about the same kid? At home he's a terror!"* This child displays two different personalities. And teenagers! They float between stoners, hicks, Goths, geeks, preps, jocks, and nerds. They switch from one part to another, like Cleopatra!

Janis Joplin

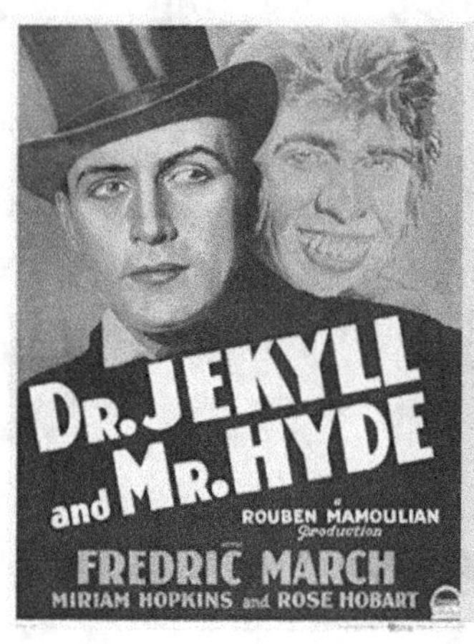

Robert Louis Stevenson
gave us that tormented soul,
Dr. Jekyll often taken over
by Mr. Hyde.

*Having multiple parts doesn't mean you've got a disorder
or mental illness. It means you're alive...like all of us!*

Three

Parts in the Extreme

*"Are you saying I've got Multiple
Personality Disorder (MPD)?"*

No. While there are similarities between what
psychologists call Multiple Personality Disorder
(MPD), and what this book describes—many parts
within us—in no way am I suggesting that we are
MPD.

In some respects we all have multiple personalities. And even though I am not an expert on MPD
and do not treat patients with that problem, there are
good reasons not to fear an MPD diagnosis.

Here's how to identify MPD (also known as Dissociative Identity Disorder, DID): MPD/DID do a hos-
tile takeover of our inner CEO. These parts, also
known as alternate personalities or alters, have
reached a level of dissociation to such a degree that
each part functions independently and often unknown
to each other, and are impervious to negotiation or
will power. MPD/DID parts have their own memories
independent of other parts.

When all parts are affected by a medical condition we call that a disease

Parts develop for good reasons. They help us
cope with unpleasant situations we experienced as
babies, small children and young adults. They help us
adapt in our family of origin and our culture.

MPD/DID parts, however, develop after trauma, horrific abuse, or other nightmarish episodes during childhood. These parts are necessary for survival
but they become polarized, frozen in time, and stuck.

The thoughts that most of us have are fleeting. MPD/DID symptoms include the thoughts that are chronic, bossy, and incredibly hard to manage. Controlling parts often is like herding cats.

Parts come and go depending on the situation. We are aware of the connection and relation between parts. Those with MPD/DID live in varying degrees of psychiatric obsession.

Think of taming your temper. Who is doing the taming? You are. What are you taming? The part of you that is angry, or jealous, or sad, or anxious. You know about your anger (or jealousy, or depression, or anxiety) and they know about you. This is normal for everyone.

Those with MPD/DID are alternately controlled by and in control of anger, but each without the knowledge of the other.

"We hates master. No! No! We loves him."

Gollum's inner parts debate among themselves.

*"Come, I say, come, not to study the map of
the realms of the sprit, but to possess it so
that you can walk freely about it and
never be afraid of getting lost."*

Jean-Pierrede Caussade, (1675-1751)
Self Abandonment to Divine Providence
Page 56

*"We don't know how you do it, but we're going to
pester you until you yield to our temptations!"*

Four

Evidence Based Therapy

"Do you trust science?

Yes. One of the most exciting discoveries made in my twenty years as a marriage and family therapist is the strategy for greater self control based on parts. It's easy enough for kids to understand and effective enough to help adults with vexing inner conflicts.

When clients describe their struggles with addiction, obsessive thoughts and conflicting desires I used to think the only thing that would help was medication. And not being a doctor, I sent them to their family physician for Prozac, Welbutrin and all manner of nifty brain helping chemicals.

A part of me felt responsible to make such referrals. But some clients were prescription averse. So another part of me was frustrated with the prescription approach. As one trained in spiritual matters of the heart I had questions—*"Why did I not see greater results with the talking cure? Was I too quick to send folks to their family physician?"*

One day I complained to myself, *"Surely there are alternative therapies that bring relief to emotional*

"IFS (Internal Family systems) is now an approved, evidence based therapeutic model."

Frank Guastella Anderson, MD (Harvard psychiatrist and psychotherapist), quoted in a PESI workshop, **"Internal Family Systems Therapy"** Lynnwood, WA., 3/11/16.

problems without medication."

Lest anyone think I'm anti-medication, the next time I have a kidney stone I'll take Oxycodone over counseling any day! And of course, I still send clients to their doctor as needed.

These questions launched an earnest quest for additional clinical counseling practices that help hurting folks. With scientific and spiritual-values glasses on I read lots of books and filtered out the chaff from the wheat (see bibliography).

The most influential author was Richard Schwartz, a family systems therapist who made the amazing connection between family members' roles, and how inner psychic parts function in similar roles.

It is common knowledge that inventors with zero interest in spirituality come up with amazing discoveries—from the Salk vaccine to the Brooklyn Bridge, from Euclid's geometry to the Hoberman Sphere—I happily to learn from anyone.

Psychologists not only have hearts and minds but they study hearts and minds all day long.

As I continued to read I began to see parallels in the "parts" approach to my reading of Hebrew wisdom literature, particularly the book of Proverbs. The sages made observations about nature (ants and weeds in Proverbs 6:6 and 24:32) and history (human relationships, power structures, philosophical thought

"Everyone has the experience of willing in a way that is contrary to other choices they have already made or ones that should be made."

Dallas Willard
Renovation of The Heart, page 145.

experiments) and they jotted down their insights.
They wrote things like:

- *"Lady Wisdom gives people the ability to come up with witty inventions"* Proverbs 8: 12, KJV.
- *"The purposes of a person's heart are deep waters; but one with understanding draws them out,"* Proverbs 20:5.
- *"The words of a gossip are like choice morsels; they go down to a person's inmost parts,"* Proverbs 18:8; 26:22.
- *"The lamp of the Lord searches the spirit of a person; it searches out the inmost being,"* Proverbs 20:27.
- *"Many are the plans of a person's heart but it is the Lord's purpose that will prevail,"* Proverbs 19:21.
- *"Better a person who controls his temper than one who takes a city,"* Proverbs 16:32.
- *"Above all else guard your heart for it is the well-*

*"What's in the heart comes
out the mouth."*

PART II

Controlling Our Parts

Five

Separating Our Parts

Self control begins with the creative acts of separating and then naming the parts of our heart. Naming parts helps us know what we're working with.

When we think about it, "self control" really is an oxymoron. Who is controlling the self? What is the self that is being controlled? Those are the questions

"The heart has reasons reason knows not of."

Blaise Pascal (1623-1662)
Penees

we will answer in this chapter.

Be advised—while my definitions are widely embraced by scholars, there is not universal agreement on what a part is or what it does. I and my clients have found this simplified conceptualization helpful but I am aware there are other ways of defining parts of the heart.

Pre-scientific, ancient writers attached temperament functions to certain body parts. They thought kidneys controlled personality traits, as did bowels (of mercy), blood, liver, spleen, gall bladder, and bones. Arms, hands, palms, hair, and loins all had poetic and symbolic meaning.

This was true for the heart as well. We all know the heart is a blood circulation pump and not the seat of the soul or home of the emo-

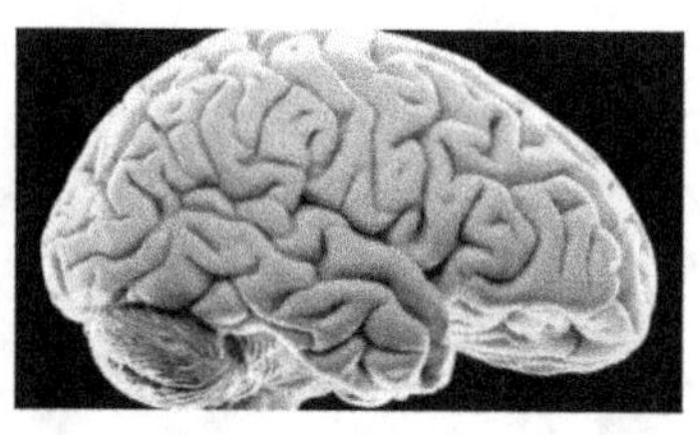

tions. Those functions originate in the brain. Heart transplant recipients do not become new people like they would with a brain transplant! For continuity's sake, I continue to use the word heart but be aware that I'm really talking about brain functions.

The heart is an umbrella term which includes many features: the will (decision making), soul, spirit, feelings (emotions), desires, motives, attitudes, passions, and a host of other intermingled personality components.

To keep things simple let's say the heart is comprised of two main domains: the soul and the spirit. These words are metaphors for what is an amalgamation of blurred functions in our understanding of inner world. Christian thought claims there is a division between soul and spirit.

There is also a division of labor in the heart. Our spirit is the invisible and immaterial domain where the real us dwells, our core self, what Dan Seigel calls the *"embodied and relational self-organizing emergent process that regulates the flow of energy and information."* That's a mouthful, but potent.

It's the center of our being, like the Chief Executive Officer of your life. For the less spiritually inclined, it could also be known as the pre-frontal cortex. I like to think it is from this spiritual place that:

- *"rivers of living water flow from within us"* (John 7:38).
- *"we participate in the divine nature "* (2 Peter 1:4).

- *"a good man brings good things out of the good stored up in his heart,"* (Luke 6:43,45).
- *"the love of God shed abroad in our hearts,"* (Rom. 5:5).
- *"the whole body is filled with light--when our eye is single"* (Matthew 6:22).

As love flows from our spirit it conquers more and more of the soul.

Within the soul are various purposes, attitudes, desires, urges, feelings, decisions, passions, cravings, images, thoughts, motives, memories, intents, and so forth all bent toward self preservation and not always altruistic. One thing all parts have in common, a wariness of following the spirit (your core self).

Parts are both discrete (different and independent of each other) and connected (one part affects the others). They are emotional, communicative, and have different ambitions. Some are wounded and need protecting, others are demanding and boss us around.

Others have desires in direct opposition to other parts. Some parts are lazy, some are driven, some

*"No jogging today, guys. I'm trying to
break this stubborn will power of mine."*

are grandiose, some are shaming.

Trauma survivors display parts when they make extreme, sudden, and dramatic shifts from calm to terrified, from relaxed to thoughts of self harm, from politeness to rage. Radical mood swings are parts at polar opposites (as in bi-polar disorder).

I was a youth pastor for many years and I'd often notice that teens who visited our youth group would make new friends with peers who shared their values. Like an invisible radar teens with common values would find each other: jocks to jocks, nerds to nerds, saints to saints, and stoners to stoners. They'd join forces without anyone orchestrating or arranging such connections.

Parts do the same thing. The guilty part hooks up with the self critical part and together they beat up on the spirit something fierce. The lonely part hooks up with the entitled part and all resolve to avoid temptation flies out the window.

Like the TV show Survivor, these parts form alliances. They join forces, form teams, com-

> *"There are times when I look over the various parts of my character with perplexity. I recognize that I am made up of several persons and that the person that at the moment has the upper hand will inevitably give place to another. But which is the real one? All of them or none?"*
>
> Somerset Maugham (1874-1965)

bat other teams, and try to kick each other out of power. Until they trust your core self, your spirit, few of them want your core self to be in charge.

Most of us have had racing thoughts and felt overwhelmed at times. Some inner parts jostle for control for months or even years. Even that giant of church history, St. Paul, experienced this. He wrote, *"I do not understand what I do. For what I want to do I do not do, but what I hate I do….. wretched man that I am!"* (Romans 7:15, 24).

I have good news for folks battered and beat up by unruly parts. Your inner self has the skill and authority to conquer the inner chaos.

Your spirit is like an orchestra conductor trying to get all the musicians to work in concert.

Or to change metaphors, your spirit is like the captain of a ship and your parts are like sailors trying to kick the Captain out. It's a mutiny!

But the Captain can tell the mutinous sailors, *"Get your grubby mitts off the steering wheel of my ship!"*

As a therapist one of my goals is to help clients unleash their inner power and learn the skills necessary to manage all their parts, bring order out of chaos of soul, mood, attitudes, fear, lies, thoughts, memories, and character. My role is to train clients to be their own therapist and conflict mediator, to tame their inner chaotic and conflicted parts.

Six

Uniting Our Parts

Mediators help two people in conflict negotiate with each other and reach a resolution.

Therapists help individuals with two parts in conflict negotiate and reach resolution with themselves. In this chapter I'll show you the reader how to do this on your own.

An individual's polarized parts say things to each other and to the individual that are extreme, unhelpful, discounting or invalidating. Parts can get stubborn, misread other parts, mistrust the spirit, mistrust spiritual values, have distorted thinking, can feel vulnerable, get easily angered, afraid, or defiant. Parts that don't cooperate with the spirit can, to use a technical phrase, *"drive us crazy!"*

Abe Lincoln said, *"A house divided against itself cannot stand."*

This is true for nations and true for our many parts. One of the goals in our counseling office is to

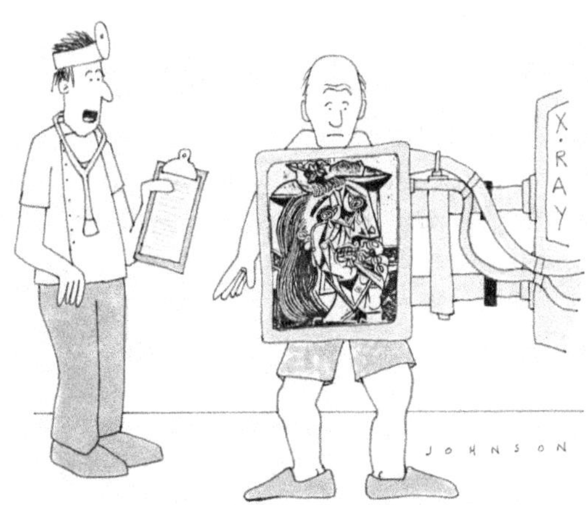

help people unify their disparate parts and bring self control. It is to our advantage to get these parts to cooperate with each other. Here's how we do it.

1. Get in touch with your inner parts. I've done this for myself and have come up with about thirty recurring and predominant parts in my heart that require managing. Jot down answers to the following questions.

- How often do you hear yourself say, *"I part of me wants ____, but another part doesn't?"*
- Which parts control you?
- Describe the self critical dialog in your head that shames and berates you. That's not your spirit talking but an inner part.
- What are some of the monologs going on inside your head?
- Where does our mind drift when we've got free time?
- Which parts do you already control?
- What parts do you cherish?
- Which parts bug you?
- What are the different ways you act around different people? List them.

Look at the list to the right; circle parts that sound familiar.

Types of Parts

Helpless
Nurturing
Rational
Logical
Stubborn
Rebel
Negative
Enabler
rumbling
Disputing
Compliant
Helper
Observer
Punisher
Entitled
Aggressor
Numb
Manager
Reactor
Self hating
Guilt ridden
Angry
Lonely
Dutiful
Critical
Nice
Pleaser
Healer
Controller
Martyr
Manipulative
Curious
Learner
Risk taker

2. Separate the parts of your soul from the real you, your spirit.

To practice self control we need to separate our soul from our spirit. To do this, give each part that listed in Step 1 a person's name. This is for practical reasons; it helps you keep those parts separate from your spirit and from each other. The soul is a busy place and it's easy to get parts mixed up with each other. Pick a neutral name. Do not pick your own name since this is only a part of us and not the real us, our spirit.

Some of my parts and their names:
- Charlie: Self doubt, self critical, insecure.
- Bob: Dutiful, responsible, workaholic.
- Rita: Addicted to books and learning.
- Simon: Craves success as a therapist.
- Cicero: Faith in providence, values the sacred.
- Hamm: Humorist, light hearted, joker.
- Amos: Non assertive and non confrontational.
- Ury: Peacemaker, mediator.
- Chuck: Creative, inventor.
- Anti-fog: Explainer, simplifier, coach.
- Scrooge: Money worrier.
- Jack: The fundamentalist cop in my head.

There are more but these are the ones I engage the most.

3. Strengthen your spirit.

When the parts of your soul are is under the control of your spirit you're integrated, calm, passionate and compassionate, courageous, connected, confident, capable and creative. In Christian thought this condition is called whole-hearted or pure-hearted.

When our spirit is overtaken by hard to manage parts of our soul the result is double mindedness and burdened.

There two ways to control our soul. Weaken the grip of those bossy, unruly parts. Strengthen the power of your inner spirit, your core self.

To strengthen your spirit answer these questions.

- Who is the boss of my life—my spirit or my soul, my core self or my parts??
- What does your spirit say to those parts?
- What should it say?
- What do your core values say to your parts?
- What spiritual disciplines have given you the most strength?
- What prevents you from exercising more of those disciplines?

4. Interview the parts.

Now that our spirit has been separated from our soul and the parts of our soul have been named, let's talk to them. Remember when Woody in **Toy Story** talked to the objects hiding under the dresser in Sid's room? He said, *"C'mon out, little fella!"*

That's what the sages meant when they said, *"Many are the purposes of a person's heart but one with understanding draws them out."*

You're going to say to your parts, *"C'mon out little fella!"*

Discovering the purpose of our parts is very interesting! Listen to how we talk to ourselves about our looks, injustices, fears, what other's think of us, the importance we place on being right, the part that reacts when we're in imaginary danger, the *"Boo!"* voice that terrorizes us.

These are not our spirit talking but parts of us.

In role play fashion, we let each part say what's on its mind. As the interviewer, you're going to win their trust, give them a voice, and listen to them. We treat them as valid, even those that are problematic. Instead of avoiding, ignoring, or pretending they don't exist, we respect them as individual parts of us. See Part IV for worksheets of questions, Take notes or have another ask the questions and you take notes.

5. Negotiate with them.
As we know, parts come in varying degrees of resistance. Some parts offer low resistance to our core self. These we can negotiate with and control without much effort. Other parts offer medium resistance. These parts require gentle persuasion. Still other parts offer high resistance to our spirit. They require stern demands to comply with our values. Then there are parts in outright rebellion.

- What is each part up to?
- Do they have any good motives behind their behavior?
- Are the parts trying to protect, soothe, warn, nourish, comfort, or punish us? Why?
- If they are extreme, what would it take to get them to back down?
- Convince unruly parts to stop rebelling with the enticement of joy; when all you parts get in alignment eve-

 Erik Douglas Johnson

ryone feels better.

- If parts are sad what do they need for comforting?
- Don't avoid or turn away from the hurt parts but embrace them.
- If parts are unruly and be assertive, *"I'm the boss so back down!"*
- What parts have allied themselves with other parts? Divide and conquer. What parts are at odds with each other?

*Jules Feiffer, **Jules Feiffer's America** (Alfred A. Knopf, New York, 1982), page 210.*

Don't be intimidated by stubborn parts. If a person said to us what our parts say to us, we'd probably just ignore them or argue back. Yet when our parts beat up on us, scold us, treat us poorly, we often cower and yield.

Why? Why do we give more power to our inner voices than they deserve? Because those nasty voices are often an echo from the past. We heard those negative and critical voices in our family of origin, past friendships, or past marriage, and the negative messages stuck.

*"I can't stand it when
I don't get my way!"*

Mr. Hippocampus

*"Remember the last
time you got riled?"*

Mr. Left Temporal Lobe

*"Good grief. Here
we go again."*

**Mr. Hypothalamus
Pituitary Adrenal
Axis**

*"No, no!! Please
don't do it!"*

Mr. Frontal Cortex

*"What are the short
and long term
outcomes of going
ballistic?"*

**Mr. Right
Temporal Lobe**

*"Let's lash out,
act out,
drop out!"*

Ms. Amygdala

"Got any other options?"
Ms. Anterior Cingulate Gyrus

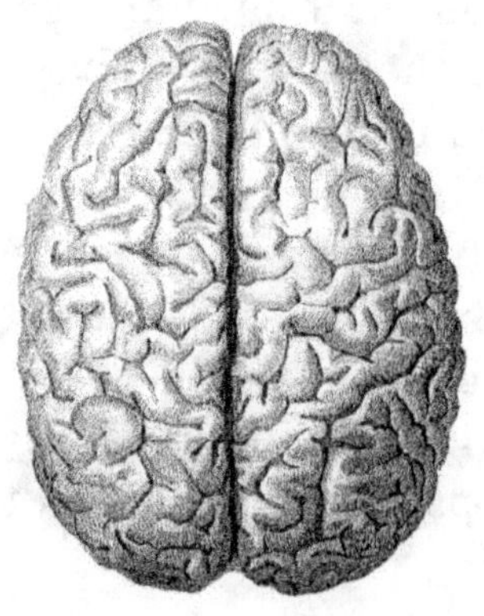

6. Get tough with them.

The point of this process is not to obliterate the parts of our heart but to bring them in all their variety under your control. We want to be whole, multi-talented, with many personality traits for different roles, etc.

However, if the conciliatory approach fails, and our parts are unrelenting, we must work smarter.

As is often the case, some parts serve the role of protector. They know there have been hurts in the past that are unhealed. They therefore do all they can to prevent you from being hurt again. They manage and prod you to be a perfectionist, controller, people pleaser, care taker, conflict avoider, worrier.

Other parts jump into action once pain has been triggered. These want to numb your pain by prodding you to act out with eating disorders, cutting, suicidal thoughts, substance abuse.

"You should have seen this group before
we started to manage our hearts!"

Annie Murphy Paul
The Cult Of Personality Tests, Page 221.

Other parts carry the wounds from the past and they are terrified to come out so they stay in the shadows, our of sight and out of mind. But there they lurk with their woundedness—shame, guilt, abuse, neglect, and so forth. It's this wounded part (or parts) that motivate the other parts to protect or pacify.

*"Think of this as an invitation to
marry me and all my inner parts!"*

Trying to appease some uncooperative inner parts in hopes that they'll back down is like throwing meat to a lion hoping it'll become a vegetarian.

Do not say, *"Okay, I'll yield to this temptation one more time," "This will be my last indulgence. Tomorrow I quit!" "If I feel this way it must be true!" "I just can't control these obsessions. I concede defeat."*

We spend time protecting that which is valuable, right? Many inventions are designed to protect our valuables—safes, bank vaults, safety boxes, insurance, locks, smoke detectors, seat belts, security systems, motion detectors. Because the heart is so valuable we do well to guard it by building the self control that prevents unruly and difficult parts from taking over.

Erik Douglas Johnson

PART III

Specific Issues

Seven

Parts Work in Action

A teen age girl who named several of her parts, "Cupid," "Ms. V," and "Fury" once said in my office, *"My Cupid part who wants to be loved and my Ms. V. part who wants to be popular have joined forces. They recruited Fury (anger) and talked me into cutting myself. They've been running me and not the other way around."*

It wasn't the real her, her core self, her spirit, who brought that temptation for self harm, it was several parts of her. The realization that it wasn't her but her manageable parts caused her eyes to light up. This was the breakthrough she needed to get hope on the road to recovery from self harm.

You've heard of defense mechanisms. That's a convenient name for parts in you that resist compliance with your core self. To woo defensive parts into cooperation I'll ask you to role play, *"Pretend you're the defensive part and I'll interview you. Answer my questions as you think that defensive part would answer if it were a separate individual."*

Once the weirdness of such a suggestion wears off, let's start the interview. Since it's easy to trigger defensiveness in stubborn parts, I maintain an attitude of empathy and respect.

1. *"May I have permission to chat with you, Mr. Defensive Part?"* I'm trying to win their support and confidence. I am pretending that the part I'm talking to is in fact a real person with his/her own ideas, opinions, fears, etc.

2. *"Why are you so determined to manage (the reader)?"*

3. *"What are you trying to protect (reader) from?"* Often it's a fear, pain, worry, or wounded part that feels

vulnerable and needs defending.

4. *"I need your help in understanding how to heal the wounded parts safely. Would you be willing to work together with me?"*

5. *"What part of (reader) are you protecting?*

6. *"What feelings do you have about life, stress, habits, etc?"*

7. *"Do you believe that (reader's) wounded parts will be wounded forever?"*

8. *"Are you tired of trying to protect (reader's) wounded part?"*

9. *"We have a common goal—something good for (reader). We just differ in what it is or how to get it."*

10. *"What would it be like to introduce to me your wounded parts?"*

11. *"What regrets do you have for not protecting (reader) in the past?"*

12. *"What role do you play in leading other parts to trust (reader's) core self?"*

13. *"What value might there be in facing your sadness and fear?"*

14. *"What kind of person do you think (reader) would like to become?"*

15. (After the interview): *"Will you agree that nothing harmful happened during this interview?"* As you learn what defiant parts are up to, you learn what strategies are necessary to get them cooperate. Therapists or writers do not have access to a person's innermost parts, but you do.

What astonishes clients when they do this role play is the insight they get into why those defensive parts have been such bullies. They're trying to help!

> *"We are not unified; we often feel that we are, because we do not have many bodies and many limbs, and because one hand doesn't usually hit the other. But, metaphorically, that is exactly what does happen within us. Several subpersonalities are continually scuffling: impulses, desires, principles, aspirations are engaged in an unceasing struggle."*
>
> Roberto Assagioli (1888-1974)

"My lust part is merely trying to cure my loneliness." So we address loneliness and render the need for lust irrelevant."

"My fear part is trying to protect me from making bad mistakes in the future." So we address the lie that mistakes are to avoided at all cost and the value of faith when facing risks.

"My self critical part sounds just like my critical parent." So we address forgiveness, boundaries, and moving on.

Other clients have acting out parts. Those parts that prompt high risk behaviors—affairs, drug use, lying, gambling, cutting, rage, and more. Using a Hebrew invitation, *"Come now let us reason together"* I invite you to role play those parts.

One guy said, *"You want to talk to my lust? I've been trying to avoid it for years!"* I asked how successful he'd been and he said, *"Not very."*

So I invited him to try an interview as an experiment. Here are the questions I asked Mr. Lust.

1. *"Your willingness to risk damaging (client's) marriage as well as triggering his guilt takes courage. What are you up to?"* Mr. Lust said *"(Client) never felt close to his mom and porn fantasies comfort him."*

2. *"I admire your good motive to bring comfort to (client). But isn't what you're doing rather extreme?"* Mr. Lust agreed it was.

3. *"Could you redirect your power and courage toward healing the lonely parts without looking at porn?"* Mr. Lust agreed to try.

The success of this interview method is that threats, restraints, and warnings often aggravate stubborn parts. Instead, we're trying to help your acting out parts understand their role and find a more useful role in your world. For parts that do not cooperate so easily, we gently earn their trust.

"If you don't do your job of protecting (you the reader), *what are you afraid will happen?"*

"If we could find you a new job would you be interested?"

Benefits of the role play method are twofold. First, you'll differentiate your unruly parts from your core self. The fear, or lust, or guilt, or anger is not the real you. Those are only hard to manage parts that will soon be managed.

Second, you learn how to talk back to unruly parts on your own. By showing respect, you'll discover what each part wants or fears, and by being direct and honest you can get their attention and (hopefully) cooperation.

Weakening the unruly parts is only half the equation. Strengthening your core self is the other half.

1. How do you feel toward a certain part?
2. Why do you think it behaves a certain way?
3. How often do you hear from it?
4. How much influence does it have over you?
5. How would you like the relationship with it to change?
6. What would life be like if your parts didn't have such extreme roles?

A woman client had been dominated by a fearful part we called Ralph (a neutral name with no significance). Ralph wanted to protect her *"from getting walked all over again so she not be hurt again."* Ralph hammered her with obsessive thoughts, *"You never know what will happen. Don't be optimistic, you'll be hurt. Don't hope for the best. Your husband is probably cheating on you."*

We differentiated the real her from the part Ralph. This was her first step in disengaging from the fears that dominated her. I told her, *"You can have these conversations without my help. You have what it takes to manage all your parts."* She was on the road to recovery. Her enthusiasm with this process was the first ray of hope she's had in ages for vic-

"Be not angry that you cannot make others as you wish them to be, since you cannot make yourself as you wish to be."

Thomas a Kempis (1380 - 1471)
Imitation of Christ

tory over her fears.

This heart was drawn by a teenage girl and illustrates beautifully the concept of mending parts. She labeled her parts *"Torn, Waiting, Searching, When? Broken, Lonely, Patience, Why?"*

If you look closely you'll see that some of the parts have been reattached, other parts are still disconnected. Seeing her reattach those disconnected

> *"It makes little sense to talk about a single 'self' when we consider that both the adaptive unconscious and the conscious self have regular patterns of responding to the social world."*
>
> Timothy Wilson, **Strangers to Ourselves**

parts was a joy, both to her and to me!

Eight

Stories

Self Condemnation

Somewhere in my misspent youth one of my parts picked up the lie, *"Real men know how to fix plumbing leaks."* It's a nutty idea, really. And my core self knows it's nutty. But as a home owner my parts don't know it's nutty.

One day our toilet sprung a leak at its base and I called a friend, *"What do I do?"*

"It's easy," he said. *"Go to the hardware store, buy a two dollar wax ring, disconnect the toilet, insert the wax ring, and reattach the toilet."*

I did just as he said but when I reattached the toilet it leaked. My self critical part whom I call Charlie whispered in my heart, *"Idiot!"*

It was only a two dollar part, no big deal, so I drove back to the hardware store, bought another wax ring, and went through the procedure again. Wax ring number two also leaked. Charlie in my soul said, *"Ha! I knew you couldn't do it."*

I ignored him the best I could but my blood pressure was rising. Wax ring number three—bought, installed, misaligned and it leaked, too. By this time Charlie was yelling, *"You are such a wimp! Any guy can fix a toilet! You are not only a bad plumber, you are a poor excuse for a male."*

Things went from bad to worse while installing wax ring number four. I'd disconnected the toilet again, it was standing in the middle of our tiny bathroom, and I accidentally knocked it over. When the ceramic toilet crashed into our bathtub the toilet broke in two.

My two dollar project was now a one hundred dollar disaster and Charlie went wild, screaming in my ear, *"Fool! Nut job! Sorry excuse for a human!"*

I know Charlie was getting through to me because my wife said, *"Erik, I'm taking the kids and leaving while you fix the bathroom. You're so angry it's upsetting them."*

Hiring a plumber would have fixed the toilet but not Charlie. It would take a stronger intervention to fix Charlie. Self condemnation and critical parts stalk us, waiting to pounce any chance they get.

The solution was to replace the lie my wounded part clung to with truth, *"Real men control their temper and plumbing has nothing to do with it. Your worth as an individual does not depend on your performance."*

A woman client once lamented, *"I don't have two thoughts in my head, only one—self criticism."* Ethel, the name she chose for that part, constantly said things like, *"You're a bad woman, bad wife, bad mother, bad employee and you can't even load the dishwasher right!"*

I explained that her core self was not bad but loaded with competencies, gifts, compassion, and so forth. The problem was that the voice in her part Ethel, was louder. I said, *"Next time you hear from Ethel, talk back to her, 'I'm okay. Beat it, Ethel.'"*

When she returned the next week she was beaming. *"For the first time in 40 years I talked back to Ethel. I messed up at work and as Ethel was starting to rake me over the coals I talked right back to her and she backed down. I'm astonished and happy!"*

What she did with Ethel is what I did (and continue to do) with Charlie. I calmed down, bought a new toilet, installed it using that fourth wax ring, and finally got it installed correctly.

Do you think that silenced Charlie? Not at all. He still dogs me when cars break, printers jam, and fuses burn. Instead of listening to his shaming messages I say, *"Charlie, you're a liar. My manhood doesn't depend on the absence of the Mr. Goodwrench gene. Get lost."* And it works.

Fear

A teenage guy was doing homework in his bedroom when his little sister, dying for attention, started bouncing a basketball against his door. The guy yelled at her to stop it but she didn't. He yelled again, and she didn't stop.

Finally, in a fit of rage he flipped out, opened the door, screamed at her, *"I'm going to kill you!"* and chased her down the stairs. Mom and dad were horrified at his outburst so they brought him in for anger management.

I asked him, *"Tell me about the incident. Why the outburst?"* He told me the following fascinating story.

"I was working on an important school project. I thought that if my little sister kept distracting me I'd get a bad grade. If I got a bad grade, I'd get a low GPA. If I got a low GPA I'd not get into college. If I didn't get into college I'd end up living on the street like a bum."

I said, *"So you weren't really trying to kill your sister but protecting yourself from a terrible fate as a homeless guy?"* He said yes.

The solution for this guy was to name and then challenge the fear part that exaggerated, extrapolated, and made a catastrophe of his future. That, plus some problem solving skills. And for mom and dad to correct the irritating little sister!

 Erik Douglas Johnson

Grief

A mom brought a 13-year-old girl to my office who began having outbursts. She'd yell at her mom, *"I hate you! You're the worst mom in the world!"*

Mom was stunned at her daughter's uncharacteristic anger, eruptions, frequent flying off the handle, and tears. It turns out that her anger was the daughter's way of managing her grief. Her older siblings had moved out and dad had gotten a job out of town. This girl's predominant inner part was grief. She named it Jerry and the conversation went like this.

Jerry to 13-year-old: *"It's your fault everyone is leaving. Life will never be the same. You should be ashamed of yourself. You're disgusting!"*

13 year old to Jerry: *"I am NOT the reason they moved out, I am NOT disgusting, I am NOT bad, just sad, and I can manage this."*

Two years later I ran into her mom who told me, *"My daughter is doing great! She's still using the skills to talk back to Jerry."*

Panic

A 25 year old woman visited our office suffering from hyper sensitivity to her husband's moods. If he raised his voice one decibel she'd panic. If he got even mildly irritated she'd react with her own anger and a frenzy of irrational thoughts. And when her young children defied her she went into panic mode—rapid heart beat, spacing out, paralyzed.

I learned that she was a survivor of childhood trauma; sadly, her parents had been incredibly cruel. This client had been suicidal at age 7, anorexic in college, and, according to her husband was, *"A high strung, high anxiety wife."*

To clam herself down she tried to change her husband, withheld sex, made demands, controlled the money, nagged, withdrew, got angry, overreacted, blamed others and then clammed up. It wasn't working.

We separated her many parts from each other and from her core self, listed them, and worked with them one by one. Some of her parts
    • Albert (incapable): *"My happiness depends on what others do."*
    • Anna (fear): *"You can't even imagine what bad things are going to happen to you! I am the Captain of your soul! I make you react for your own protection!"*
    • Doug: (irresponsibility): *"I am not making ANY negative contributions to this marriage."*

> *"It is the rule of thumb among cognitive scientists that unconscious thought is 95% of all thought—and that may be a serious understatement."*
>
> Robert Burton, **On Being Certain**, page 237.

• Jill (self loathing): *You're fat and ugly."*

As her core self was strengthened, the grip of these terrorizing parts weakened. She learned to talk back to each one and gradually her symptoms decreased.

• To Albert she'd say, "*I am not hopeless or helpless!*"

• To Anna she'd say, "*Whatever may come God will take care of me and my family. Stop pushing my adrenaline button! And guess what? You are NOT the Captain of me!*"

• To Doug she'd say, "*I must stop blaming my husband and be a kind and loving wife.*"

• To Jill she said: "*God loves me and considers me worthwhile,*" to which she imagined Jill saying in reply, "*I can't argue with that!*"

Indecision

A pregnant teenage girl came to see me. Her question, "*Do I stay with the dad or not?*"

She had two parts pulling her in two directions. I asked her to give a name to each part and in a role play give them a voice. I asked both parts, "*What should (client) do?*"

The teenage girl pretending to speak for Kate (the part that wanted to stay with the dad) said, "*Dad may marry someone who isn't you and that woman will influence your child. If you don't marry him you won't have full control over your kid's diet, naps, or exposure to TV. If you're there you can limit the damage he'll do. Plus, you still may have feelings for him. The child would have two parents. When you both get along it's fun. You'd model to the kid a healthy couple relationship, and you could do cute things together, go to the zoo, water park, dress up."*

I must admit, Kate sounded pretty convincing to me.

Always mindful of the Hebrew Proverb, *"The first to present their case seems right until another comes and examines them,"* I asked the teenage girl to role play the part that wanted her to leave the dad.

She named that part Sam and said, *"Your friends, your parents, and even the dad himself is against the marriage. His scary, loser friends are against the marriage. He's lazy, irresponsible and immature to the max. You get bored with the dad, he makes poor choices, he plays video games all day long, he drinks to much, he lies to you, is selfish, and he's not even working. You could have someone supervise the visits."*

After listening to Kate and Sam by the end of the interview the client said, *"Yuk! I don't want to be*

"As societies have themselves differentiated (to use a sociological term) into largely separate spheres and institutions—financial, religious, artistic, commercial, familial, educational, and so on—so have their inhabitants' minds become unabashedly polymorphic.... many of us tend to shift from one mode to another, depending on what sphere of life we are reengaging in at the moment."

John Stackhouse,
Humble Apologetics,
page 32.

with him. Kate wins!"

Bad Habits

A 39 year old reading-impaired male came in saying, *"Why do I always need some addiction?"*

He had tried quitting tobacco, alcohol, porn, and street racing all without success. He was into cams, carburetors, crankshafts, big speakers, big engines, and he kept getting big speeding fines. It's my habit to give clients supplemental reading material but I knew that wouldn't work for this non-reader. So we talked.

He named his *"adrenaline junkie"* part Jack (after Jack Daniels whiskey) and in the role play the client spoke for Jack.

Jack: *"I act out to protect (client's) hurt parts. He was powerless as kid, bullied at school, controlled by alcoholic parents, accused by friends for doing things he didn't do. To give him power I make him make choices. Making bad choices is better than having no choice."*

Me: *"How do you chose what actions to take?"*

Jack: *"I make him do the very things his family disapproves of—cigarettes, booze, fast cars."*

Me: *"What would happen if you didn't prompt him to do these things?"*

Jack: *"He'd be overwhelmed with grief. When he got too big to spank his mother hit him with words. All this excitement prevents him from getting more*

"As couples label their parts they are able to see the patterns of interaction and find ways to break the vicious cycle."

Lori Gordon, **Passage to Intimacy**, page 194.

"Only those who try to resist temptation know how
strong it is. A man who gives in to temptation
after five minutes simply does not know what it
would have been like an hour later."

C. S. Lewis

hurt."

Once the client realized he'd been avoiding the
hurt parts in his heart we focused on them. When big
hulking men break down in tears I know hard work is
happening!

Jack: "I also beat him up with criticism to make
him feel incompetent. As soon as he feels competent
then there's no role for me."

The client's breakthrough moment was facing
the pain of the past—abuse, neglect, trauma, and loss
of loved ones he never fully grieved.

His battle with Jack will be an on going battle
but he's now equipped with a strategy to talk back to
Jack and nurture the wounded parts.

After one and a half months of no drinking we
terminated. "He went from being like a three year old
to a grown man," a family member told me.

"It was during a time of painful conflict that I first
began to experience myself as more than one. It was as
though I sat in the midst of many selves. Some urged
me down one path and some another. Each presented a
different claim and no self gave another self an
opportunity to be fully heard."

Elizabeth O'Connor, **Our Many Selves**, page 3.

Part IV

Conclusion and Annotated Bibliography

Eleven
Parts and Christian Thought

King David interviewed his downcast parts when he said, "*Why are you downcast, O my soul? Why so disturbed within me?*" (Psalm 42). And, "*How long must I wrestle with my thoughts and every day have sorrow in my heart? How long will my enemy triumph over me?*" (Psalm 13:2).

Since different parts have different purposes, goals, ambitions, and plans, it's important to try to understand what those purposes are.

Here's what James 3:2-5 sounds like in my paraphrase. "*We all struggle with many unruly parts. If anyone conquers all the unruly parts he is a perfect man, able to keep his whole body in check. When we put bits into the mouths of horses to make them obey us, we can turn the whole animal. Or take ships as an example. Although they are large and are driven by strong winds, they are steered by a very small rudder wherever the pilot wants to go. Likewise the tongue is a small part of the soul, but it makes great boasts. Consider what a great forest is set on fire by a small spark.*"

This passage asks us to control the inner dialog of our parts with a bit, a rudder, and a fire extinguisher!

Others in the Christian tradition used parts-like language.

St. Paul in 1 Cor. 9:21-23, "*To those not having the law I became like one not having the law...to the weak I became weak...I have become all things to all men so that by all possible means I might save some.*"

St. Paul in Romans 6:13, "*Do not offer the parts*

of your body to sin as instruments of wickedness but...to God as instruments of righteousness."

James 1:8, *"A double minded person is unstable in all their ways."*

Many Psalms invite us to get in touch with the parts of our heart: *"When you are on your bed search your heart and be silent" (4:4). "May the words of my mouth and the mediation of my heart be pleasing in your sight," (19:14)."*

"I remembered my songs in the night, my heart mused and my spirit inquired," (77:6). "Search me O God, and know my heart; test me and know my anxious thoughts. See if there is any offensive way in me," (139:23-24).

Unlike Ulysses Everett McGill who, in the movie **O Brother Where Art Thou**, said he believed in, *"all manner of lesser imps and demons and the great Satan hisself is red and scaly with a bifurcated tail, and he carries a hay fork,"* parts are not demons.

1 Chronicles 28:9, *"The Lord searches every heart and understands every motive behind the thoughts."* Hearts have many parts; here are two of them: motives and thoughts.

1 Kigs 18:21, *"How long halt ye between two opinions? If the Lord be God follow him; but if Baal, then follow him."* This writer acknowledged that people get pulled in two directions by two parts: idols and gods.

1 Corinthians 14:15, St. Paul said, *"I will pray with my spirit, but I will also pray with my mind; I will sing with my spirit, but I will also sing with my mind."* There were two parts in Paul at work, his mind and spirit.

Galatians 2:20 is confusing until we understand the "I" and the "me" are two different parts. *"I have been crucified with Christ...it is no longer I who live but Christ lives in me."*

Galatians 5:16, *"The Spirit wars against the flesh."* That sounds like parts to me.

Even Jesus said, *"The spirit is willing but the [will of the] flesh is weak,"* (Matt. 26:41).

Psalm 51:6, *"Surely you desire truth in the inner parts; you teach me wisdom in the inmost place."* Whatever that inmost place entails it's not hard to imagine God wants truth in our heart, brain, mind, motives, thoughts, attitudes, and beliefs—all the parts.

St. Paul wrote in Romans 6:19, *"You used to offer the parts of your body in slavery to impurity and to ever-increasing wickedness, so now offer those parts in slavery to righteousness leading to holiness,"* I used to think those parts were our hands, mouth, feet, eyes, etc. Then I realized that it's the parts in our heart that dictates what our hands, mouth, feet, and eyes do.

1 Corinthians 2:11, *"For who among men knows the thoughts of a man except the man's spirit within him? In the same way no one knows the thoughts of God except the Spirit of God."*

Proverbs 20:5, *"The purposes of a man's heart are deep waters, one with understanding draws them out."*

James 3:6, *"The tongue also is a fire, a world of evil among the parts of the body."* How is it that we tell ourselves to control what we say and then say just the opposite? Because the tongue has a mind of its own! Jesus again, *"Love God with all your heart, mind, soul and strength"* (Matt. 22:37). There's a list of parts for us!

Some final random wrap up thoughts
- Our goal is to integrate all our unruly parts
- It is harder to hear, *"I am angry at you"* than, *"a part of me is angry at you."*
- The core self is competent to lead once unencumbered by bossy parts.
- When parts take over the core self the role player should speak for that part, not *from* that part.

- Parts have three roles: prevent pain, soothe from pain, hide from pain.
- Protectors have two fears: *"If I don't do my job bad things will happen,"* and *"I will be stuck in this role of protector forever."*
- Parts are valuable, let's have a better relationship with them.
- We do not have a unitary mind.
- All parts have motives for why they're so extreme.
- When parts latch on to us it's a burden, like a vi-

Annotated Bibliography

Allen, David, **Ready for Anything** (Penguin, 2003). Not a book about psychology but Allen briefly describes his parts with wit and charm.

Bernstein, Peter, **Against the Gods: The Remarkable Story of Risk** (John Wiley & Sons, 1996). Our attitudes toward economics, gambling, randomness, and uncertainty are affected by parts in our soul. Christians like Pascal, Bayles, Gataker, and others played a significant role in developing principles for managing risk. Very engaging book.

Burton, Robert, **On Being Certain** (St. Martin's Press, 2002). Does the feeling of being certain arise from logic and reason? Maybe not, says Burton. Part philosophy and part neurology, this book describes a scientific theory of certitude based on biology. If the Christian belief in a spirit is not true, we're left with *"insufficient evidence to know how thoughts emerge from neurons"* (page 136). Thought provoking!

Carter, Rita, **Multiplicity: The New Science of Personality, Identity, and the Self** (Little, Brown and Company, 2008). This dandy work offers exercises on discovering our subpersonalities. The first half is theoretical and provides the latest findings on mind research.

De Caussade, Jean-Pierre. **Abandonment to Divine Providence** (Image Books, 1975). Letters from a priest to nuns in France in the 1700s.

Gordon, Lori H., **Passage To Intimacy** (Simon and Schuster, 1993). One of the more effective marriage education programs, P. A. I. R. S. (Practical Application of Intimate Relationship Skills) relies heavily on the notion of subpersonalities. Highly readable and very practical.

Goulding, Regina and Richard Schwartz, **Mosaic Mind** (W. W. Norton & Co., 1995). Exquisite (though lengthy) story of an abuse survivor dealing with all her parts. Fascinating reading. See also Richard Schwartz's other book, **Internal Family Systems**.

Hacking, Ian, **Rewriting the Soul: Multiple Personality Disorder And The Sciences of Memory** (Princeton University Press, 1995). As the title implies, this is a scholarly treatment of MPD, its history, controversy, relation to dissociation, trance states, and trauma.

O'Connor, Elizabeth, **Our Many Selves** (Harper and Row, 1971). As far as I can tell O'Connor was the first Christian to popularize the theme of multiple parts in our heart. It's a small yet helpful workbook for exploring one's parts and a collection of an astonishing number or quotes by writers advancing the notion of subpersonalities. One wonders why this book never achieved greater acclaim.

Paul, Annie Murphy, **The Cult of Personality Testing** (Free Press, 2004). The wildly popular practice of identifying our types, traits, and talents with written tests is challenged in this provocative book. As testers know, personality test results vary. Why? Because of the complex and sometime elusive nature of subpersonalities.

Paulos, John Allen, **A Mathematician Reads the Newspaper** (Anchor Books, 1995, page 111). This is where I found the Minsky quote cited on page 46.

Rowan, John, **Subpersonalities: The People Inside Us** (Routledge, 1990). This book is an early treatment of the topic intended for non-academic readers. Rowan compiled dozens of quotes of secular psychologists writers (1950s – 1980s) about subpersonalities.

Schwartz, Richard, **Internal Family Systems** (Guilford Press, 1995). Schwartz's brilliant thesis: the same systems that influence families (polarization, alliances, rigidity, over protectiveness, blending, differentiation) influence the parts of an individual. Thus, this therapeutic method for dealing with parts is called Internal Family Systems. Profound and thought provoking.

Sliker, Gretchen. **Multiple Mind: Healing the Split in Psyche and World** (Shambhala, 1992). Her not-always-easy-to-read but very interesting hypothesis: global conflict is a reflection of the conflict within individuals' own hearts. A hypothesis with which Christians should resonate.

Stackhouse, John, **Humble Apologetics** (Oxford University Press, 2002). Describes our post modern world with fragmented parts. Highly recommended.

Stone, Hal, **Embracing your Inner Critic** (Harper San Francisco, 1993). New Agey but a couple of interesting insights.

Townsend, Henry, **Hiding from Love** (Zondervan, 1991). By the boundaries guy before launching his immensely popular line of boundaries books, Townsend walks readers through the steps to coordinate our parts that need separateness while at the same time reacting to lack of attachment.

Willard, Dallas. **Renovation of the Heart** (NavPress, 2002). A magisterial work exploring all the nooks and crannies of our heart. Willard tries to keep it non academic (he almost succeeds) but it's still rich, deep, and inspiring. Highly recommended.

Wilson, Timothy, **Strangers to Ourselves** (Belnap Press, 2002). What the Bible calls our inner being, Wilson calls our adaptive unconscious. Replete with entertaining and fascinating descriptions of psychological experiments, this book explores (non-Freudian) ways in which to understand the purposes of our unconscious: evaluating our behavior and reflecting on other's evaluations of ourselves.

> *"The trouble comes when Part A says, "Do X," and Part B says, "Do Y." And then X happens, and Part B goes into rebellion. Or Y happens, and Part A feels abandoned and depressed. Fortunately, there is a CEO. The challenge is to get him to show up at the right time to take his appropriate role in high-level analysis, intelligent decision making, and assurance of appropriate implementation."*

David Allen, **Ready for Anything**, pages 103-104.

PART IV

Worksheets

The pages that follow include handouts I use with clients to help them understand, identify, and manage their parts. I am under no illusion that these charts of nonphysical realities are comprehensive or exhaustive. They might even create the impression that the parts of our hearts are tidy and easily categorized. Yet no diagram can fully capture the living interplay between soul and spirit. Nevertheless, many find these visual aids helpful. I hope you do as well.

Anatomy of the Heart

"Guard your heart with all diligence for out of it flow the issues of life." Proverbs 4:23

PARTS = a multiplicity of thoughts, desires, urges, passions, attitudes, motives, cravings, beliefs, lies, reactions, lusts, drives, appetites, defenses, memories, fantasies, ideas, feelings, etc. that determine behavior (Prov. 4:23). These parts are all tainted (some more, some less) by sin (Jeremiah 17:9). This means they don't cooperate with the Spirit (Gal. 5:17). They need reviving and restoring (Ps. 19:7; 23:3).The Bible tells us to manage them (Romans 6:13, James 3:6) with Holy Spirit power. Doing so means loving God will <u>all</u> our heart. We need divine help to do this because parts have a mind of their own!

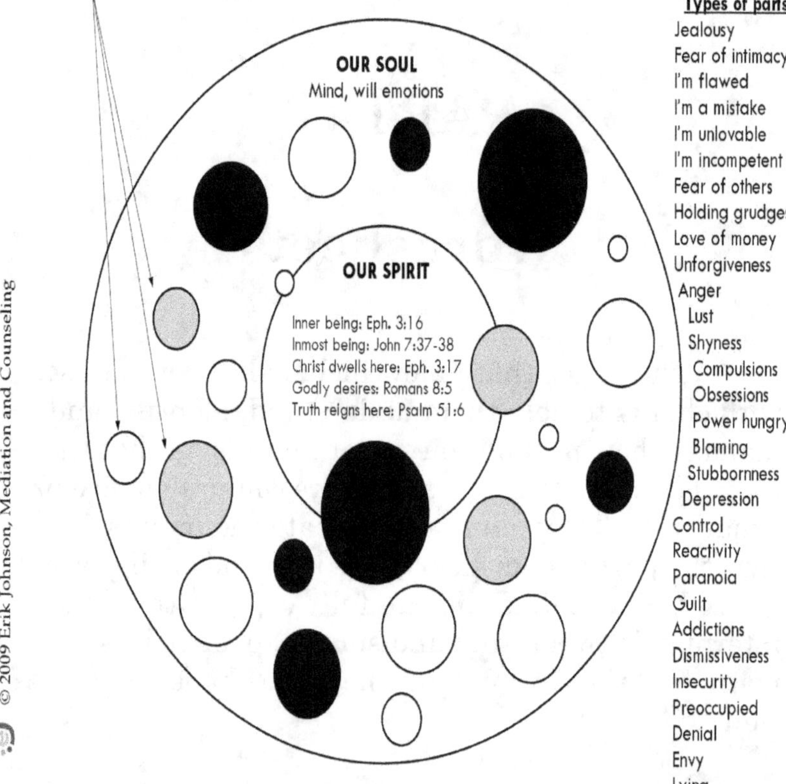

<u>**Types of parts**</u>

Jealousy
Fear of intimacy
I'm flawed
I'm a mistake
I'm unlovable
I'm incompetent
Fear of others
Holding grudges
Love of money
Unforgiveness
Anger
Lust
Shyness
Compulsions
Obsessions
Power hungry
Blaming
Stubbornness
Depression
Control
Reactivity
Paranoia
Guilt
Addictions
Dismissiveness
Insecurity
Preoccupied
Denial
Envy
Lying

Proof that parts exist

Bible: 1 Kings 18:21, Romans 7, Phil. 1:23, 1 Cor. 14:15, Psalm 77:6, Jer. 17:9, James 1:8, Ps, 86:11, Jer. 31:33; Isa. 3:17; Job 38:36, Luke 11:17

Experience: indecision (part of me wants to leave; part stay), self criticism, buyer's remorse, chorus of critical voices in our heads, the "committee," day dreaming, *"I don't do the things I want to,"* analogy: *Body of Christ and our bodies are one yet many parts*

Counselors "draw out" parts to help the us manage them better (Prov. 20:5). Our "tools" include:

Bible Heb. 4:12; Psalm 119:11
Prayer Ps. 139:13-14; Jer. 17:10; 1 Chron. 28:9
Fellowship Heb. 3:13
Reflection Psalm 4:4, 1 Cor 2:11; 4:5
Sp. warfare 2 Cor. 10:4-5

Four spheres of the self

Help Yourself and Others Get a Deeper Understanding of Who You are

Erik Johnson, Family Counselor, 384-4211

4. The Public Self: The part of us on display, the part of us that usually takes most of our time and effort (working on our appearance, hairstyle, compliance or non-compliance with social norms, pleasing or displeasing others, clothing, eye contact, voice inflection, vocabulary, etc). We manage this image with integrity (congruent with our core self) or with a disguise (fraudulent masks, false presentation, pretending). The media implies by its ads that this is of ultimate importance. How many ads address the core self: character, worth? How many ads address the public self: skin, spots, clothes, muscles, hair, etc? Like the peel of an orange, the public self is important, but not the whole of one's being. There's more to you than the way you look.

* Name ten things you like about your stomach? (good evaluation of your level of satisfaction with your public self)
* What about your public self is the real you, who you are becoming, and who you'd like to be?
* How important is it to you to fit in? How important is it for you to be liked?
* What are your unwritten rules about your public self? "I always ___ in public. I never ___ in public."
* How many roles do you have (parent, spouse, son/daughter, employee, etc). Which fits you best? Why?
* What about your public self would you like to change?

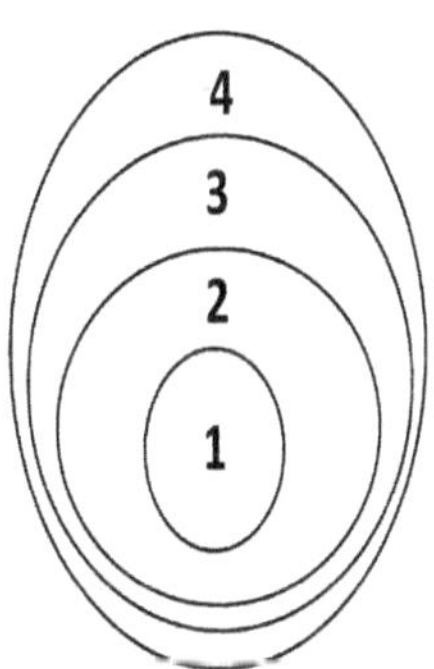

3. The Defensive Self: The strategies we use to keep people focused on level 4 and away from levels 2 and 1, that keep us away from knowledge of our flaws, that protect us from being overwhelmed with shame and guilt, and avoid exposure of level 2. Typical (conscious and unconscious) defense techniques include humor, denial, rage, withdrawal, hide, justification, over responsibility, perfectionism, addictions, and more. Assaults on level 2 and 1 may be real or imagined. Excessive uncalled for defensiveness could imply guilt and shame (Romans 2:15).

* What defenses are familiar to you? Do they work? How can they be improved?
* What parts of your public self are you trying to preserve?
* What other ways can you handle the challenges to your social and private identity?
* What parts of level 2 (flawed sense) can you learn to accept?
* What could someone say to you that would automatically trigger your defenses?

2. The Flawed Self: The part of us that is the repository of guilt and shame. The area of our life that discredits us or makes us feel defective. The part that says, "If you really knew me you'd not like me." The inner sense of self that says we're mean, disgusting, filthy, incompetent, evil, rotten, selfish, stupid, less than ideal.

* Who told you those things were bad about you? Who is telling you that now?
* What is one thing you don't want others to notice about you? What don't YOU want to notice?
* "If I weren't so busy using these defenses I would _________ (go crazy, have to get honest, be free)."
* If you had the power to change anything about you (personal qualities/features/defects) what would you change?

1. The Core Self: That part of us that answers the question, "Who am I?" "Who am I becoming?" "What is my purpose in life?" It's also known as the self image. It can be shamed, wounded, etc. How well do you accept our 10 unchangeable features (parents, sibs, birth order, race, gender, aging/death, time in history, looks, IQ, nationality)? Was your soul steeped in shame or love, worth or criticism? People who are at peace with themselves know much about this sphere.

* What is your identity? Who does God say you are? What are your passions/interests?
* Turn shoulds into coulds. "I could do ____." Who would you like to become?
* When do you use that phrase, "Well, that's just the way I am."
* What do you do or could you do that will help you develop a healthy sense of pride?
* Use the phase, "I want ___ but ____." to find hidden dreams, wishes, hungers, longings.

Identify and Manage Your Purposes, Plans, and Inmost Parts

"The <u>purposes</u> of a person's heart are deep waters; but one with understanding draws them out," Prov 20:5.
"The words of a gossip are like choice morsels; they go down to a person's <u>inmost parts</u>," Prov. 18:8; 26:22.
"The lamp of the Lord searches the spirit of a person; it searches out the <u>inmost being</u>," Proverbs 20:27.
"Many are the <u>plans</u> of a person's heart but it is the Lord's <u>purpose</u> that will prevail," Proverbs 19:21.
"Better a person who controls his <u>temper</u> than one who takes a city," Proverbs 16:32.

Identify as many "parts" of you that you can. Name them, jot down the things they tell you, discern their motives. Like an conductor who leads an orchestra, I want to help you lead your orchestra better.

Name of this part   Name of this part   Name of this part   Name of this part   Name of this part

Comments made by these parts

Our Heart
"Above all else guard your heart for it is the wellspring of life."
Proverbs 4:23

Interview Your Parts

1. May I (the <u>**Core**</u> me, the real me, my soul/spiritual being) interview you (the part)?
2. Mind if I take notes while we talk?
3. What can I do to earn your trust during this interview?
4. Would it help to assure you I don't want your demise....just to understand you better?
5. I get the impression you have a hard time following my (and the Holy Spirit's) lead. Why?
6. Is there anything I can do to earn your trust?
7. Do you understand how your pushiness and "mutiny" affects me?
8. What other parts in me align themselves with you?
9. What other parts in me resist and react to you?
10. What are your core values, Mr./Ms. Part? What's important to you?
11. What makes you tick? What desire in you will be filled when *"mission accomplished?"*
12. When you engage in wishful thinking, what do you wish for?
13. Why do you think you drive me to do the things I do? What's your motive?
14. What intoxicates you and gets you delirious with joy? What exhilarates you?
15. What are the rewards when you get (client) to act out?
16. What charges your batteries?
17. What are your ling range goals?
18. What is the "pleasure payoff" for you?
19. Hypothetically speaking, if you were to be unleashed with no regulation, where would (__) end up?
20. Conversely, if you were to exercise self control, what would be the long term pay off?
21. What would it take to regulate yourself?
22. What would it take for you to listen to the cautions of (client's) core self, the inner spirit?
23. Would you agree that because of God's presence in my life the <u>**Core**</u> me is basically calm, curious, courageous, capable and creative?
24. Would you consider yourself a part that is a **Manager** (keeping all the other parts --and my <u>**Core**</u> self-- in line), a **Wounded Victim** (hidden out of fear and self protection), or a **Reactionary Radical** (stirring up trouble)? Or other?
25. I'll be honest with you...my desire is with God's help to keep you (my unruly part) in line. How does that sound to you? Why?
26. If you are a **Wounded Victim** part, what would it take to comfort you and help you find healing? What memories do you have that bug you? Can you identify any lies you may have picked up over the years?
27. If you are a **Manager** part, what would it take for you to trust me and God and follow our lead? May I have your permission to interview the other parts? Why are you so determined to manage things? Don't you trust me? What parts of me are you trying to protect? Are you of the opinion that the wounded parts of me will be wounded forever? Why? Would you be willing to join forces with me and you "manage" the other parts to follow my and the Lord's lead?
28. If you could talk to the <u>**Core**</u> me without fear of my reaction, what would you tell me?
29. If you could talk to Jesus without fear, what would you tell him?
30. If I could talk to you and speak the truth in love, what do you think I'd tell you?
31. If Jesus would talk to you, what do you think he'd say?
32. If you're a **Reactionary Radical** part, what would it take to keep you on a shorter leash? Do you frighten me to assert control over me? Are there healthier ways you can release your pent up emotions without reeking havoc?
33. Mr./Ms. Part, how important to you is God's truth?
34. As a result of this interview, would you (the part) agree that nothing bad or harmful happened?
35. Is there anything you (Mr./Ms. Part) would like to say to Erik?
36. Mr./Ms. Part, what is it about yourself that you like? What positive role do you fill in my life?
37. What would you like to say to the wounded parts in my heart?
38. How old are you? Do you feel frozen in time? If you're stuck in history, how would you feel about coming into the present?

When Desires Take Over

Failure to keep our desires in check leads to conflict with ourselves and with others. The test of our priorities is not what we desire but how we respond when our desires are not fulfilled. What rules your heart?

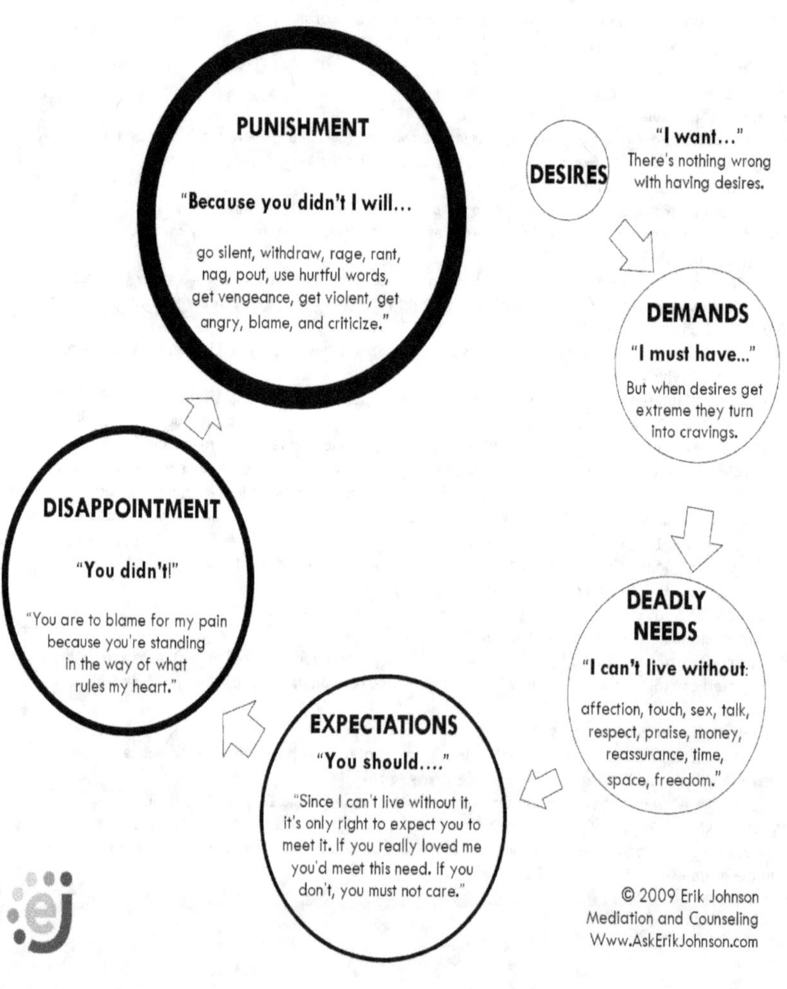

Motivating the Stubborn Parts in us to Change

Erik Johnson, Family Counselor 384-4211

If plans to make important life changes have been sabotaged by the stubborn parts in us, it's often helpful to interview that part and find out what's up, why it's preventing you from making the changes you want. Here are questions to help evaluate those "reluctant to change" parts. Start by naming the thing(s) that you'd like to change about you, your behavior or your circumstances ________________________

____

____ .

		YES	NO
1	Are there benefits to making these changes?		
2	Would making these changes move you closer to those you care about?		
3	Would making changes in your behavior move you in a direction that's good for you?		
4	Are the things that you'd like to change in your power to change?		
5	If you don't make these changes will you be worse off?		
6	Would making these changes help the people around you?		
7	Are your current behaviors helping you get what you want?		
8	Would not making these changes result in greater stress, tension or frustration in you?		
9	Do you have a clear idea of what you want?		
10	Do you think negative self talk hinders your progress toward making these changes?		
11	If you keep living the way you are will you end up at your desired destination?		
12	Are your behaviors in keeping with the rules, goals, policies of your home/job/school/church?		
13	Is there a possibility that your current troubles have been brought on by your own behavior?		
14	Are your current behaviors preventing you get what you want?		
15	If you keep living the way you are will you end up at an undesired destination?		
16	Do your current behaviors hurt those around you?		
17	Are your current behaviors going to keep you out of trouble with the law?		
18	Is your plan for change an effective one (simple, doable, achievable, measurable)?		
19	Do your desired changes seem reasonable to those around you?		
20	Do you say to yourself, "I can't change!"		
21	Are your desired changes for long term benefit rather than short term gain?		
22	Are your desired changes for short term gain rather than long term benefit?		
23	Would making these changes result in benefit to your school/home/church/job?		
24	Is there a reasonable possibility of you getting what you want in the future?		
25	Are your wants truly in your best interest?		
26	Do your behavior have a positive influence on the quality of your work (@ job or school)?		
27	Is your current view of things helpful? (sometimes we need to change lenses, not the world)		
28	Are you truly happy when you violate a principle that is important to you?		

www.ingramcontent.com/pod-product-compliance
Lightning Source LLC
Chambersburg PA
CBHW051909250726

48659CB00002B/552